Super Senses

Anita Ganeri

EXPLORE
Super Senses
See, hear, taste, smell and touch! Find out how your senses work.
OXFORD
Super Senses
OXFORD

Contents

Making Sense

How do I find out what is going on around me?

I use my **senses**.

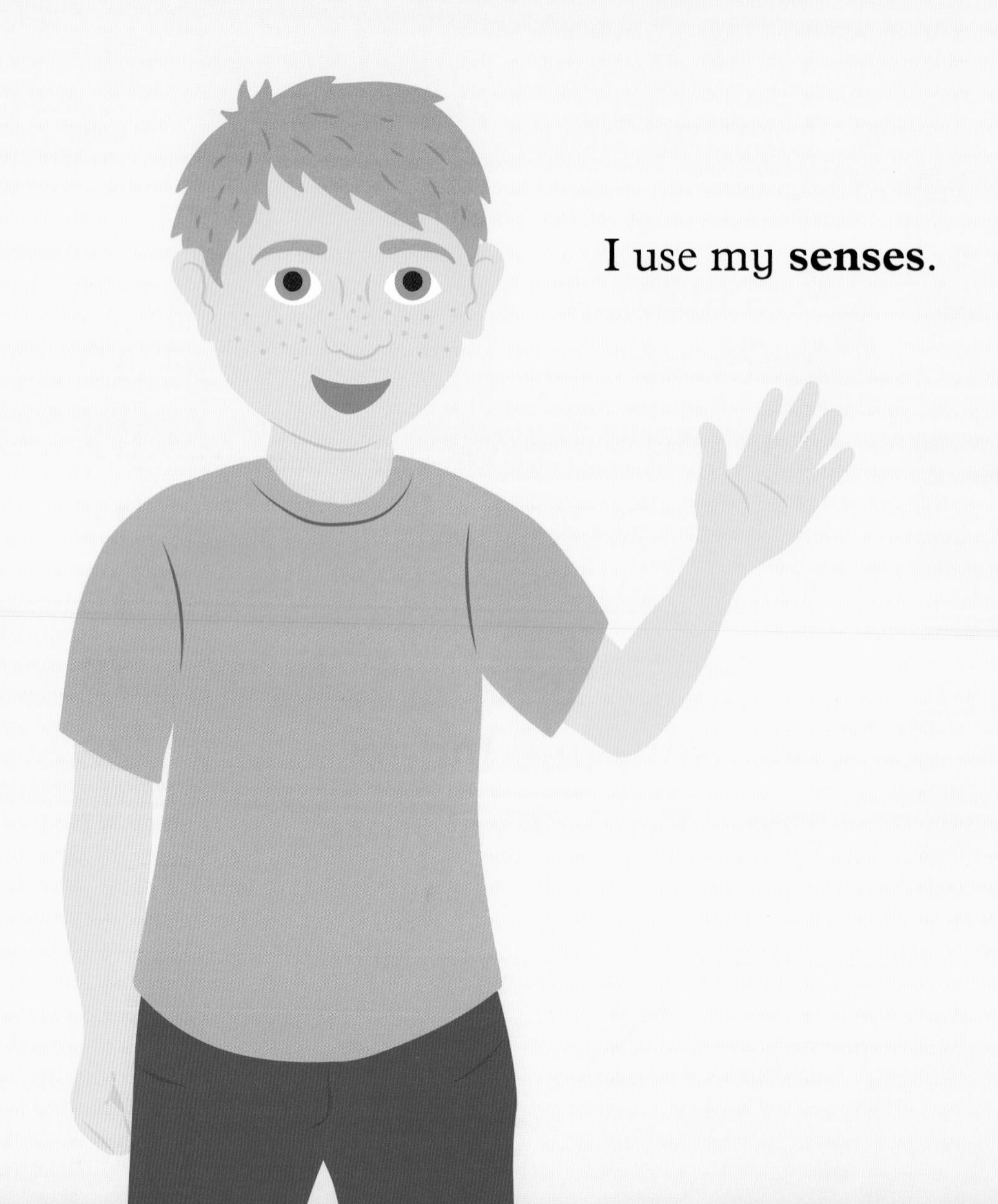

I see with my eyes.

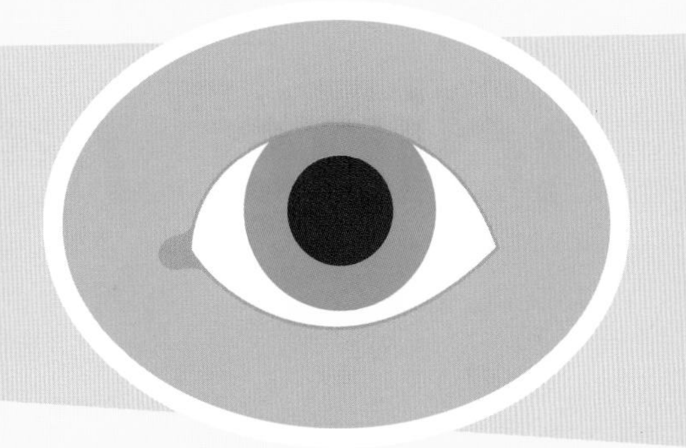

I hear with my ears.

I taste with my tongue.

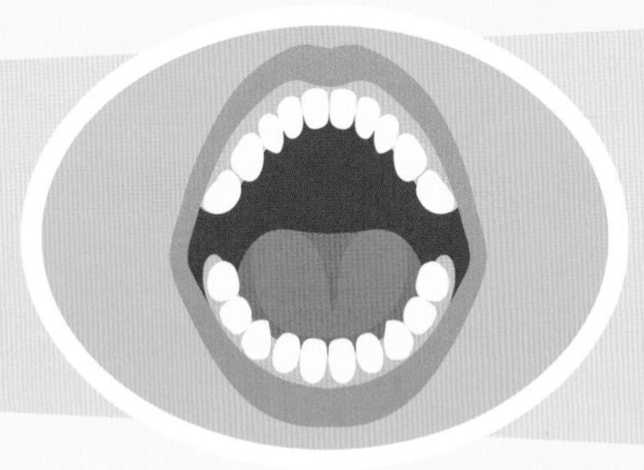

I smell with my nose.

I touch with my skin.

Sending Messages

My senses send messages to my brain.

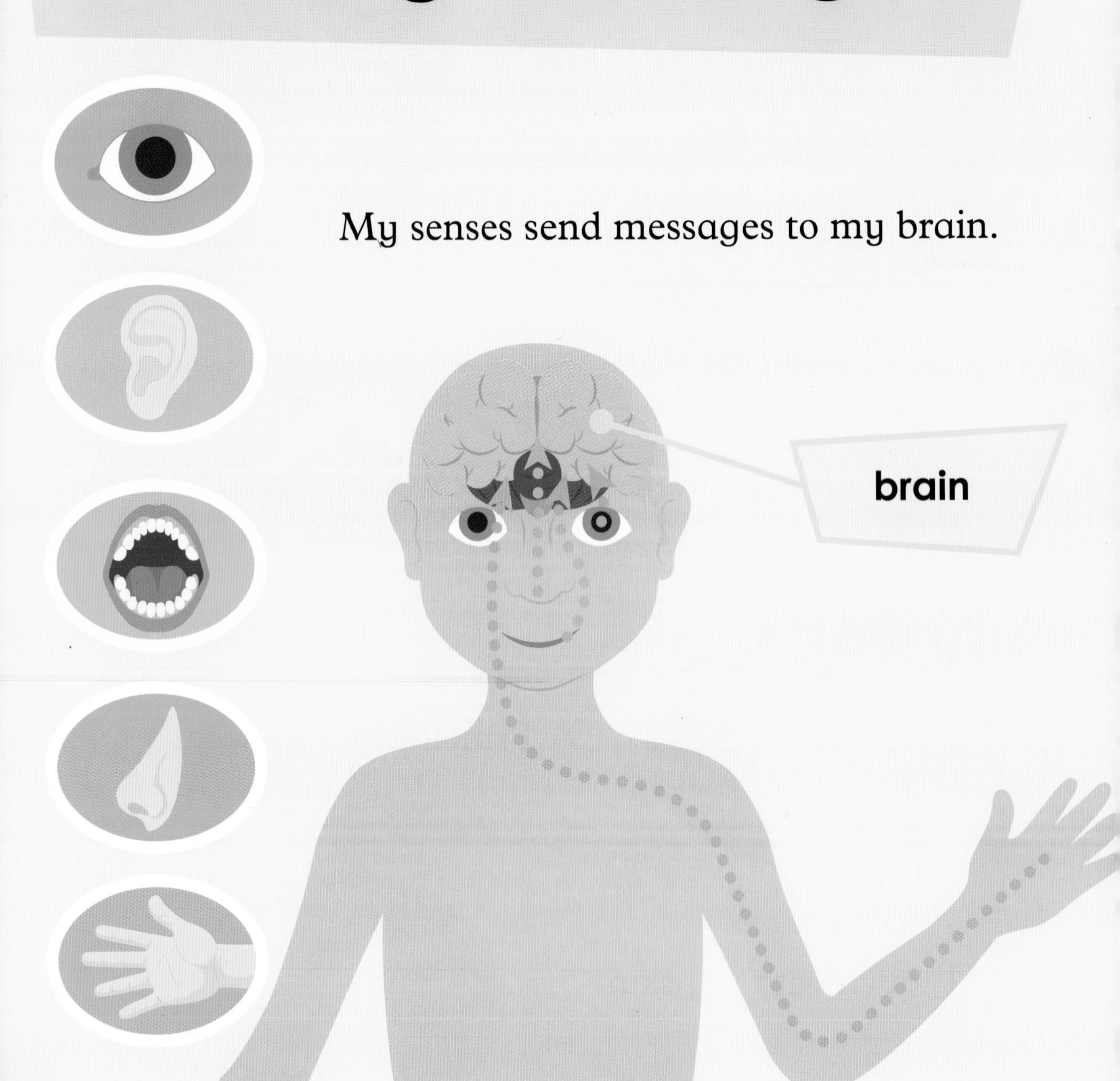

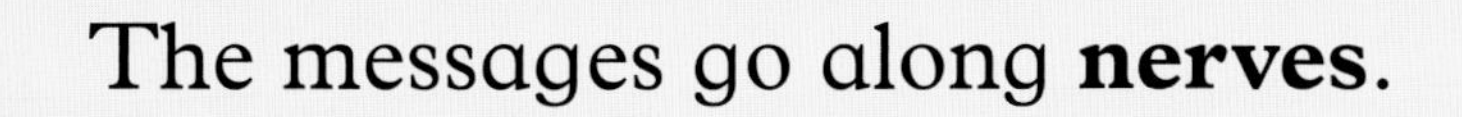

The messages go along **nerves**.

nerves

The messages from my senses tell my brain what is happening.

My brain sorts the messages. It sends messages to my body to tell it what to do.

Seeing

I see with my eyes. Light goes through tiny holes in the middle of my eyes. The light makes a picture. A message is sent to my brain. The picture is what I see.

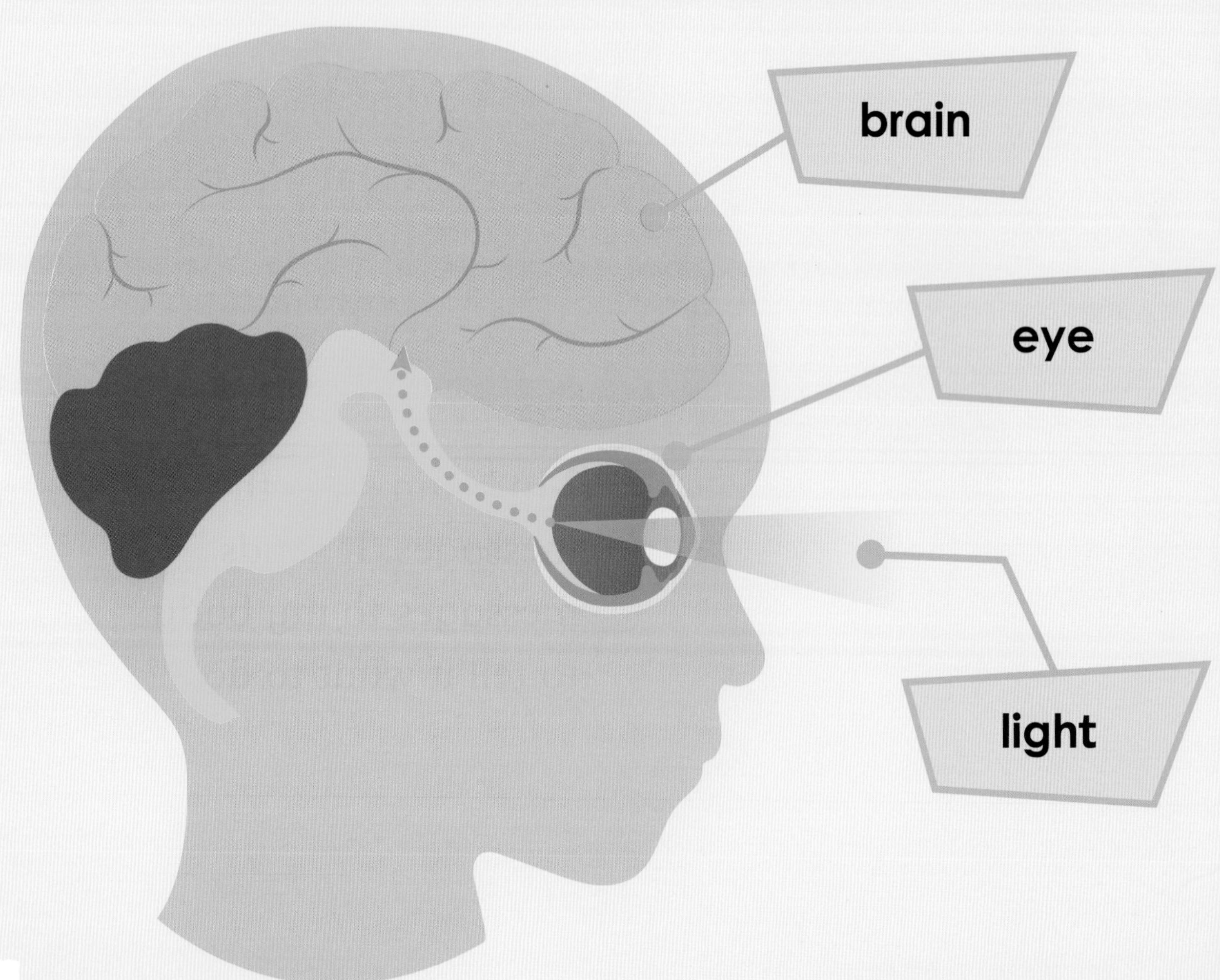

Some people wear glasses to help them see.

Glasses stop things looking fuzzy.

People who are blind find it difficult to see or cannot see.

This boy is using his sense of touch to read. He feels dots on the page.

Hearing

I hear with my ears.

Sounds go into my ear holes. Then they go along a tube into my ears.

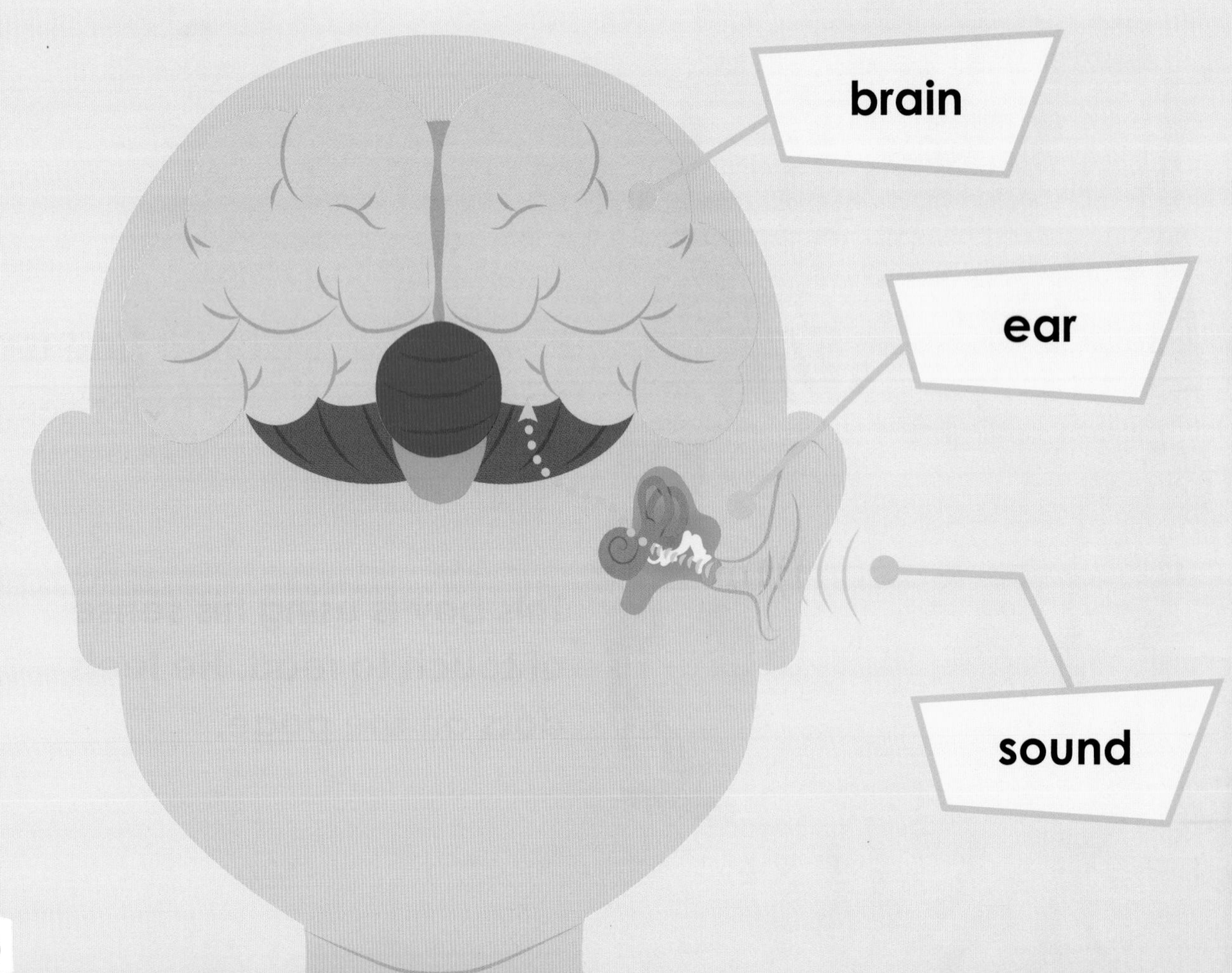

Some people wear a hearing aid to help them hear.

A hearing aid makes sounds louder.

hearing aid

People who are deaf find it difficult to hear or cannot hear.

These children are talking using their hands.

Tasting

I taste with my tongue. My tongue has lots of tiny bumps, called **taste buds**.

There are thousands of taste buds on my tongue.

When I eat, they pick up different tastes from my food.

sour taste

sweet taste

Smelling

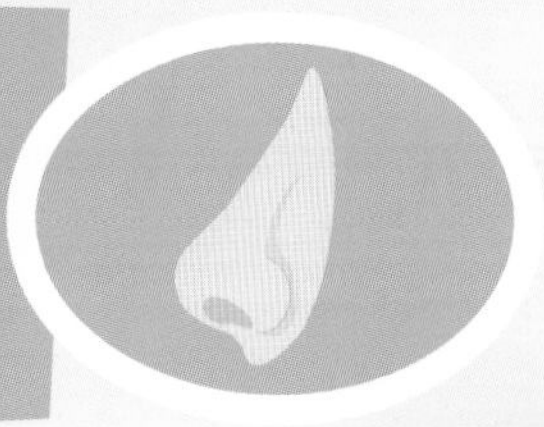

I smell with my nose.

When I breathe in, smells from the air go up my nose.

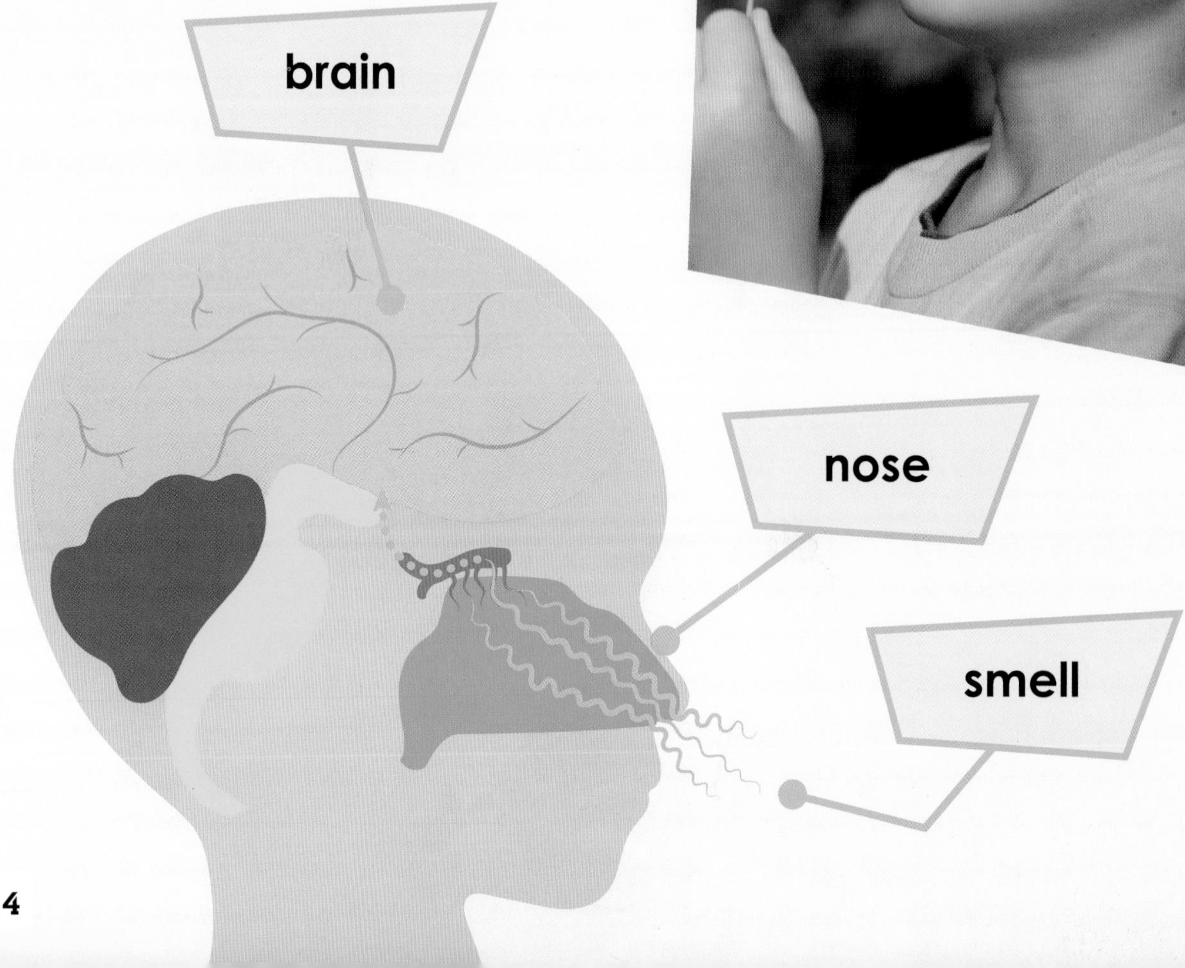

My nose helps my tongue to taste my food.

If my nose is blocked, I cannot smell. This makes my food taste different.

Touching

I touch and feel things with my skin. My skin tells me if things are hot, cold, soft or hard.

The skin on my hands is good at feeling. When I stroke a cat, it feels soft and furry.

A message is sent from the skin on my finger to my brain.

Animal Senses

Some animals have excellent senses.

Seeing

A **tarsier** has huge eyes for seeing in the dark. Each eye is as big as its brain.

Hearing

Bats have very good hearing. Some can hear an insect walking on a leaf.

Tasting

A butterfly doesn't have a tongue. It tastes leaves with its feet. If the leaf tastes good, the butterfly lays eggs on it.

Smelling

Snakes use their tongues to smell. They flick their tongues in and out to get smells from the air.

Glossary

nerves: parts of your body that carry messages to and from your brain

senses: the main senses are sight, hearing, taste, smell and touch; you use your senses to find out what is going on around you

tarsier: a small furry animal that lives in trees in the rainforest

taste buds: tiny bumps on your tongue that you use to taste

Index

Look Back, Explorers

What are the bumps on tongues called?

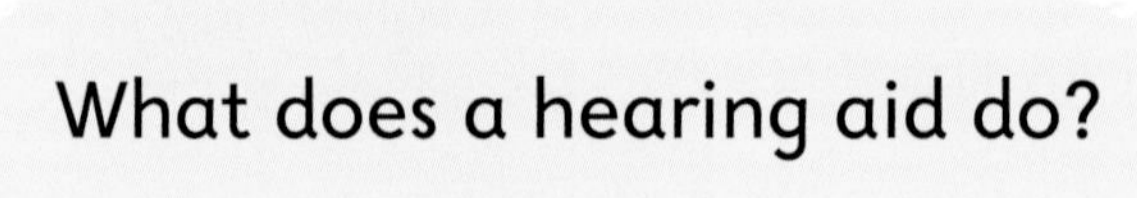

What does a hearing aid do?

Re-read page 8. How do you see with your eyes?

A cat feels *soft and furry*. Can you think of any other words to describe how it feels?

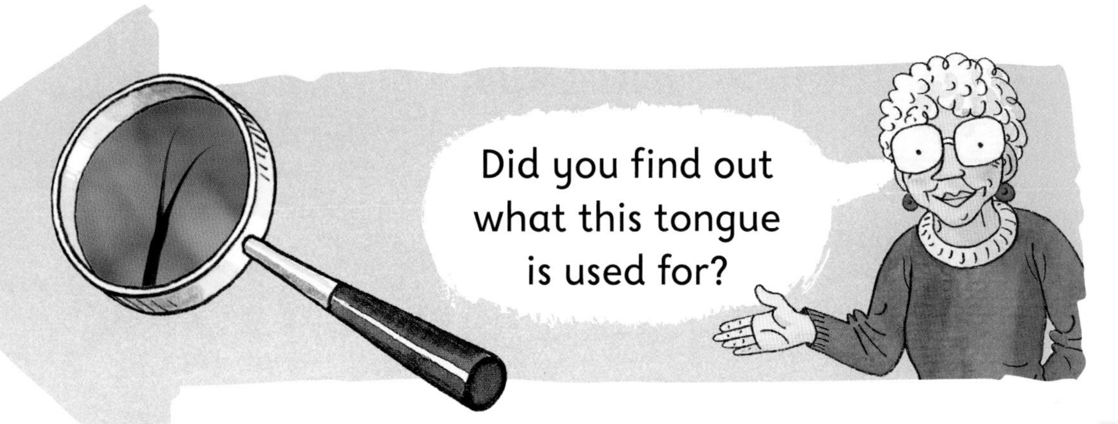

Did you find out what this tongue is used for?

Explorer Challenge: to smell (page 21)

What's Next, Explorers?

Now you know about your senses, find out why Biff and Chip need to see in the dark ...

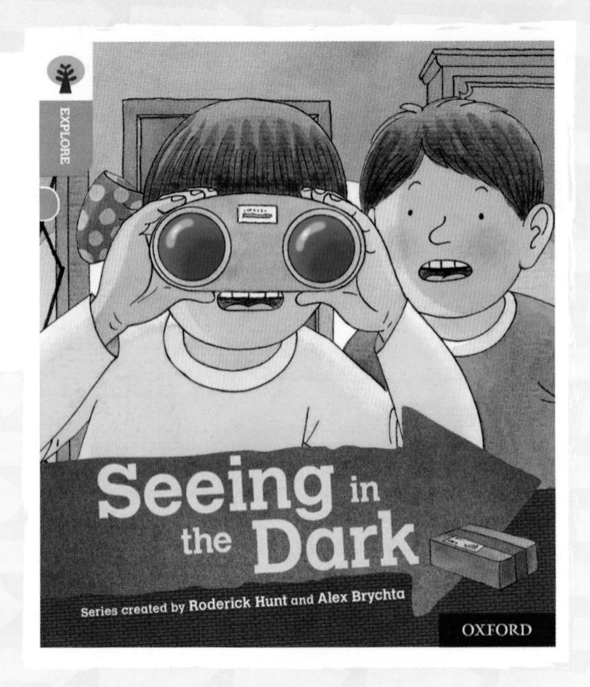

Explorer Challenge
for *Seeing in the Dark*

Find out what is sniffing this mushroom ...